JOHANNI

The Man Behind the Printing Press

Copyright © 2018 by Henry Freeman.

All rights reserved.

Table of Contents

Introduction
Living in the Medieval World
Gutenberg's Early Childhood
Gutenberg in Strasbourg
The Printing Press
The Printing Method
Impact of German Movable Type Printing Press
Gutenberg's Printed Books
Later Life and Death
The Legacy of Johannes Gutenberg
Conclusion

Introduction

We all love to stay in touch. For anyone reading this book, and for most others, staying in touch is easier than ever before. No longer do we have to communicate on cave walls or write long, descriptive letters to get our point across. Now, it's just a click of our instant message icon on our smartphones, and we get to say all we want to just about anyone across the globe.

Communication with the written word has been going on since time began. Even the ancients knew how to convey their messages using written symbols. Eventually, this led to the formation of alphabets and more sophisticated forms of correspondence. Over time several significant innovations followed, such as the telegraph, the telephone, and the internet, all of which have transformed societies.

Each of these discoveries made it that much easier to reach out and touch someone. These inventions have been like ripples on a lake; when you throw in even the smallest of pebbles, they make an impact. Depending on where you are standing you may feel the full splash or you may not even get wet. In today's world, there are still people who know nothing about text messaging or websites.

For our purposes, we need to look at the Middle Ages. Tucked neatly in between the Fall of Rome in the fifth century and the Renaissance, the Middle Ages was a period of almost a thousand years. The early centuries of the Middle Ages were often referred to as the Dark Ages.

However, there was nothing dark about this time. One of the brightest lights that would shine in these years was that of Johannes Gutenberg. Born in modern-day Germany, he started life as a blacksmith, goldsmith, printer, and then something entirely new to the world in which he lived—a publisher.

Let us have an in-depth look at how Johannes Gutenberg came to invent his printing press. First, we need to see the world during his time; how similar it was to ours, but also how vastly different.

Chapter One
Living in the Medieval World

"For three hundred years we have had our focus on the individual. We have distinguished him from the objective world as the Middles Ages did not think of doing. We have given him the world and the universe as a playground for exploration and discovery."

—John Grierson

Today, we live in a modern or even post-modern world. Looking back at history, we can learn about different civilizations and time periods by separating them into eras. Go to any college or university, and you're sure to find courses on all historical time periods. The only problem with studying these as past history is that they all take on a very one-dimensional outlook. There are dates, events, and names. The trouble is, you never really get to know the people who were living in these times.

Living in medieval times was very different from how we experience life today. Europe would be unrecognizable for a twenty-first-century person; most countries, like France, Germany, and Poland, were small kingdoms or duchies which all fought for the same king. The Middle

Ages would come to change this outlook by helping countries see their identities as individual nations.

In earlier centuries, the seventh and eighth, countries were trying to hold themselves together without the protection of the Roman Empire. These countries realized they had a struggle ahead of them; there would no longer be any outside help. As the decades and then centuries progressed, many European countries were finding their inner strength through this trial. The one significant unifier in all of this was the Roman Catholic Church.

The Church played a huge role in the Middle Ages for nearly every European country. It was hard to find to find anyone in Europe who was not deeply influenced by the Church and its doctrines. During this time in history, there was no other significant religion in Europe.

In the decades leading up to the birth of Johannes Gutenberg, there were some significant events which would change the course of European history. The one event which superseded the rest was the Black Death. Also known as the Great Plague, this sickness reached the shores of Italy in about 1348. The deadly disease started spreading quickly, and no one knew why or where it came from.

Giovanni Boccaccio, an Italian writer and poet, gives us an idea of how the plague manifested itself, "In men and women alike it first betrayed itself by the emergence of certain tumors in the groin or armpits, some of which grew as large as a common apple, others as an egg. From the two said parts of the body this deadly gavocciolo soon began to propagate and spread itself in all directions indifferently; after which the form of the malady began to change, black spots or livid making their appearance in many cases on the arm or the thigh or elsewhere, now few and large, now minute and numerous. As the gavocciolo had been and still was an infallible token of approaching death, such also were these spots on whomsoever they showed themselves." Usually, this was followed by a high fever and vomiting of blood. Most victims died two to seven days after their initial contact with the disease. This first, great outbreak of plague in Europe wouldn't be the last. Every few decades, there would be another flare-up, and people would flee as fast as they could.

Figures for the death toll are estimates at best. It is believed that the plague killed between 75 to 200 million people in Eurasia. In some countries and cities, as many as 40-60% of the population perished. Everyone was affected. It didn't matter if you were a peasant, shop-owner, judge, nobleman, lady of the manor, priest, bishop, monk, or king. The plague ravaged through Europe, making its way through Italy, into the German states, until it crossed the waters to England. Travelers would come upon villages where the whole community was wiped out and lying dead, covered in erupted boils on their skin.

In time, the plague set Europe on a collision course with the Church and gave its survivors the strength to challenge social, economic, and religious beliefs. Living in the Middle Ages, people did not have the sense of self we have today. We have hopes and aspirations; we dream big. That is a luxury which was not afforded in medieval Europe. Most people were tied to the land in some sort of serfdom. Unless you were an educated member of society, you worked until you died; you had little in the way of options or desires.

Individualism wasn't necessary in medieval Europe. From the king and his knights, nobles, and others who served him, all the way down through the ranks of shopkeepers, businessmen, and the peasants, there was no need to reach out and be different. The thought had yet to cross anyone's mind.

Religious beliefs were strong and held by most people, there was always some form of persecution going on around you, and death and destruction were often right around the corner. Life was short and could be grisly. There was no wasting time thinking about "me."

Most people were illiterate. If you were lucky enough to have a life in the Church, then you were highly educated, but education for the rest was thought to be a waste of time. Tradesmen and craftsmen were prevalent in every town, and business was conducted through the guilds which ruled over all.

Life in the Middle Ages was highly structured. There was a place for everyone, and everyone knew their place. Besides, there wasn't much room to protest or bring attention to oneself.

By the 1370s, the Great Schism in the Church would eventually lead to the ordination of three popes instead of one. For a time, the papacy was moved out of Rome and into Avignon, France. What started out as a religious feud grew into conflicts which would divide Europe. Suddenly, secular leaders were gaining prominence and would take center-stage in the events which would unfold in the coming decades.

In the 1380s, some were brave enough to start speaking up and voice their opinions. In England, John Wycliffe started a movement against the Catholic Church, and the Peasants' Revolt was brought on by the never-ending war with France and the high taxes which were being imposed on the people.

Imagine having survived the worst sickness ever to befall humankind. Members of your family are probably dead, certainly most of the town you lived in and many higher figures of authority. You go to bring your season's harvest to the lord of the manor, only to find that he's dead too, and there is no one running any manor any longer.

It would be forces such as these, even though not initially successful, which would put the idea of individualism into people's minds. All they needed was a way to express themselves and to get their word across. As usually happens when there is a need, someone rises to meet it—that someone would be Johannes Gutenberg.

Chapter Two

Gutenberg's Early Childhood

"The tendency to gather and to breed philosophers in universities does not belong to the ages of free and humane reflection: it is scholastic and proper to the Middle Ages and to Germany."

—George Santayana

When Johannes Gutenberg was born, sometime around the year 1400, there were no telephones, TVs, cars, roads, refrigerators, air travel, telegraph, and certainly no internet. You walked to get where you had to go; few people had the luxury of a mule or a horse, as they were reserved for the upper classes. Life was dirty, and you probably wouldn't change your clothes or take a bath very often. It was also short because there was no penicillin to fight illness, no surgery that would successfully help your condition, and no dental care.

Most people were toothless by the time they were in their thirties, most women died in childbirth due to different complications, and most children did not live to see their fifth birthday. All you had on your side was your faith, and people understandably clung to it like gold.

It was into this world that Johannes Gutenberg was born. His year of birth is not officially known; it is thought to be between the years 1394 and 1404. In the 1890s, even without a birth certificate, Gutenberg's birth date was declared to be on June 24, 1400.

Born in the old city of Mainz situated on the western bank of the river Rhine, Johannes was the youngest son of an upper-class merchant, Friele (Friedrich) Gensfleisch zur Laden, and his second wife Else Wyrich, who was the daughter of a shopkeeper. There is no baptismal certificate, but it is assumed that Gutenberg was baptized somewhere close to where the family lived. Most of his early childhood is a mystery, and little is known about his activities.

The name Gutenberg was derived from the house inhabited by Johannes' father and his paternal ancestors, "zu Laden, zu Gutenberg." His father worked with the episcopal mint, which meant he had to be literate in order to retain his acquired knowledge and technical skill in metalworking. This, no doubt, was passed on to his son.

As a young boy, Johannes loved to read. Handwritten manuscripts, or rolled scrolls, had already been replaced by block-printing. The printer would cut a page-sized block of wood and cut out the individual words that would be needed for that block. The wood from the sides of the letters would be cut away, leaving the raised letters. The ink was applied, and the paper was pressed down upon the printer's block. This method was extremely time-consuming, yet it was faster than copying manuscripts by hand as the monks had done centuries before. As with most conveniences of the day, books could only be bought by the wealthy. Gutenberg became determined to figure out a way of making books available to the general public.

In 1411, the Gutenberg family moved from their hometown of Mainz because of an uprising against the richer families. The Gutenbergs most likely moved to Eltville am Rhein (Alta Villa), where Else had an estate she had inherited. Johannes' older brother would stay in Eltville for the rest of his life. Eltville would become one of the first towns to experience book printing. With his family remaining there, Johannes would travel to Strasbourg where new connections were waiting for him.

Chapter Three

Gutenberg in Strasbourg

"I have often called attention to the fact that walking through the streets in the Middle Ages was a different experience from nowadays. Right and left, there were house facades that were built out of what the soul felt and thought. Every key, every lock, carried the imprint of the person who had made it."

—Rudolf Steiner

Little is known about Johannes Gutenberg's life for the next 15 years. Finally, in 1434, one of his letters appeared indicating that he was living in Strasbourg where he had become a goldsmith. When Gutenberg moved to Strasbourg, his sole dream was to come up with a way to make printing easier and faster. It was simple enough to find a room in an abandoned monastery where he worked on his project during the day.

Three years later, Johannes seems to have been instructing a wealthy tradesman on polishing gems, but where he acquired this knowledge is not known. In court records of 1436 and 1437, Gutenberg's name also comes up in connection with a broken promise of marriage to a woman in Strasbourg, named Ennelin.

In 1439, Gutenberg was involved in making polished metal mirrors for sale to pilgrims in Aachen, a city nearby. These mirrors were believed to capture holy light from religious relics, and that same year the city of Strasbourg was exhibiting its collection of relics from Emperor Charlemagne. Because of a terrible flooding, however, the exhibit was delayed for one year.

In the meantime, Gutenberg had investors to repay. All his money had been used up, so Johannes told his lenders that he would let them in on a secret he had been working on. Most speculate that this idea was Gutenberg's printing with movable type.

Working in medieval times was a bit different from how we work today. You didn't just go out and look for a job; what you did was find someone who would apprentice you, and you would learn a trade. Blacksmithing, stone carving, textile workers, glassmakers, masons, merchants, weavers, spinners, and the like. You learned a craft when working with a master craftsman, and when you were old enough, say 12 or 13, you would become a journeyman and work as the master craftsman's assistant. Guilds were the only way to secure work in medieval times. There were merchant guilds and craft guilds, and all guilds were very powerful in the cities themselves. After all, they were the ones who set the standards for skill, established guidelines for trade, and all other aspects that dealt with their business.

Once a journeyman, you were getting paid for your work. As long as you continued learning your craft and paid your craft dues, you were well on your way to becoming a master craftsman of your own. When you look at all the magnificent cathedrals of Europe, they were all built by master craftsmen and their apprentices.

Johannes Gutenberg was a member of the goldsmiths' guild. He taught his pupils—Hans Riffe, Andreas Heilmann, and Andreas Dritzehn—about gem-polishing, the manufacture of looking-glasses, and the art of printing. Many young master craftsmen were backed by generous patrons, and Johannes was no different.

During the 1440s, Gutenberg was still working on his printing press, and it is said that he had perfected and unveiled the secret of printing, all based on his own research. There is little evidence to tell exactly what he was working on or even if some early trials using movable type were conducted in Strasbourg.

Chapter Four

The Printing Press

"One of the stories I love is how Gutenberg's printing press set off this interesting chain reaction, where all of a sudden people across Europe noticed for the first time that they were farsighted, and needed spectacles to read books (which they hadn't really noticed before books became part of everyday life); which THEN created a market for lens makers, which then created pools of expertise in crafting lenses, which then led people to tinker with those lenses and invent the telescope and microscope, which then revolutionlized science in countless ways."

—Stephen Johnson

It is presumed that Johannes Gutenberg left Strasbourg by 1444. He moved back to his hometown Mainz, and he was coming very close to perfecting his movable type printing press as evidenced by the fact that his brother-in-law, Arnold Gelthus, lent him 150 gulden in the year 1448. It is thought Gutenberg used this money for printing paraphernalia.

By the late 1440s, Gutenberg is believed to have perfected the art of intaglio printing. Intaglio printing is a printmaking technique in which the image is incised into a surface, and the incised line or sunken area holds the ink. This method is the direct opposite of a relief print.

By 1450, things seemed close to lift-off. Gutenberg had formed a close relationship with a wealthy citizen of Mainz, one Johann Fust. A young goldsmith and lawyer, Fust had become interested in Gutenberg's endeavors, and he offered to become the young man's patron. Fust loaned Gutenberg 800 guilders to establish a printing plant and buy all the supplies needed.

By this time, the printing press was in operation, and Gutenberg had already printed a German poem—possibly the first thing printed using his new printing press. Peter Schoeffer, who would become Fust's son-in-law, also wanted to join the enterprise. He had previously worked as a scribe in Paris and knew quite a lot about some of the very first typefaces ever made.

Chapter Five

The Printing Method

"The information highway will transform our culture as dramatically as Gutenberg's press did the Middle Ages."

—Bill Gates

The 800 guilders that Fust had loaned Gutenberg was just what he needed to continue experimenting. One of the better things Gutenberg did was to switch from wooden type to metal type. This allowed him to make more progress. His workshop was set up at a property which belonged to a distant relative. No one knows when Gutenberg decided on publishing the Bible as his first big project, but in order to do this he needed more money. So, once again, he persuaded Fust to give him another 800 guilders. By 1452, he was hard at work on his first new project.

In order to make some money off of his printing press, Gutenberg was also publishing other texts, ones which were more expensive. These were most likely Latin grammars. Some historians have speculated that Gutenberg had two presses; one for his Bible project and one for everything else.

One of the many things which were printed on Gutenberg's press were thousands of indulgences for the

Catholic Church. These prints have been documented in 1454-1455. In the Middle Ages, the Catholic Church ruled everything and everyone. If you disagreed or tried to challenge their authority in any way, you were summarily dismissed, probably in the form of excommunication. For most people, keeping Church commandments and living good Christian lives was all they wanted to do. As the years progressed, indulgences became increasingly popular in the Middle Ages as a reward for displaying piety and doing good deeds. Faithful Catholics wanted the Church to give indulgences for the saying of their favorite prayers, doing acts of devotion, attending places of worship, and going on pilgrimage.

Unfortunately, the abuse of indulgences was becoming a bigger problem every day. Those working for the Church, and even those who weren't started selling indulgences to the public. Many indulgences promised complete salvation from eternal damnation; something everyone had on their mind all the time. No one wanted to burn in Hell for all eternity, and suddenly there was a way of getting around it.

Now, with Gutenberg's printing press, indulgences were being printed by the thousands. Unbeknownst to Johannes Gutenberg or anyone else at the time, these indulgences would grow to such proportions that by the beginnings of the sixteenth century an obscure priest by the name of Martin Luther would unleash on the world an event which would tear the Church in two.

So how exactly was Gutenberg able to print the indulgences and other documents in such rapid succession? He had a specific method. Printing can actually be seen as far back as 3000 BCE, in early Mesopotamian civilizations. Round seals were used for rolling an impression into clay tablets. In China and Egypt, small stamps were used for sealing, and these were followed by larger blocks. In China, India, and Europe, cloth printing came before paper or papyrus printing.

Printing with a press was used in Europe during the Middle Ages. By 1300, printing on cloth was used all throughout Europe. Then around 1400, paper began to be relatively easy to obtain, and printing transferred to small woodcut religious images and playing cards which were printed on paper. By the year 1425, these prints became very popular.

This method of printing, known as woodblock printing, also utilized block-books, which were woodcut books that contained both text and images. Everything was carved in the same block of wood and became the bestsellers of their day. These block-books appeared in Europe between 1440-1460, and some historians claim they preceded movable type printing while some historians say they came after.

Movable type printing is the system of printing using movable pieces of metal type which use matrices or metal molds for casting a letter. Every letter, every symbol, every everything used in movable type printing was created as a metal mold. Sometime around the year 1040, the first movable type system was created in China out of porcelain. The inventor, Bi Sheng, also invented wooden movable type, but used, instead, clay movable types.

Neither system was widely used, one reason being that the Chinese character set is immense. Metal movable type began to be developed in Korea where, by the fourteenth century, the world's oldest extant book to be printed with movable metal type was created. This form of movable metal type was very similar to the one eventually used by Gutenberg.

The East's method of movable metal type may have spread to Europe between the late fourteenth century and early fifteenth century. Gutenberg is credited with developing European movable type printing by the 1440s. Along with Gutenberg, there were also minor players such as Johann Fust and Peter Schoeffer, who experimented along with Gutenberg in Mainz.

When one compares woodblock printing to movable type printing, the movable type was faster and longer lasting. Letters cast in metal were going to last a good while longer than those fashioned out of woodblock. Because of this, lettering became more uniform, which made it easier to create better typography and led to the development of different fonts.

The Gutenberg Bible proved to the world that movable type printing was the way of the future. Once Gutenberg's printing press was established, many printing presses were quickly being set up all throughout Europe.

Chapter Six

Impact of German Movable Type Printing Press

"I wouldn't be surprised if history records Tim Berners-Lee as the second Gutenberg."

—Stephen Johnson

Believe it or not, the Bible was not the first published work of Johannes Gutenberg. Sometime around 1450, Gutenberg began preparing his Bible project to move forward, but it wouldn't be until 1454 or 1455 that the first finished copies were available. Instead, the first datable printing of anything ever printed by Gutenberg is Gutenberg's 31-line indulgence. Issued on October 22, 1454, the 31-line indulgence was a plenary indulgence granted by Pope Nicholas V. Indulgences came in different forms and could be either plenary or partial. To gain a plenary indulgence, a person must not commit any kind of sin going forward, even small sins like venial sins, and must perform the work or say the prayer for which the indulgence is granted.

This datable printed work doesn't show anywhere on its face who the printer was or where the printing took place. It is assumed that Johannes Gutenberg printed the document using the D-K type and that it was printed in the city of Erfurt, which was in close proximity to Mainz. The year of 1454 is printed on the document using movable type, and there is a blank space on lines 18 through 21 where the month, day, and name of the person buying the document can be filled in by hand.

There were three important changes which Gutenberg made to his printing process. The first sheets were rubricated by being passed twice through the printed press, using black ink then red ink. This didn't work well and was soon abandoned, leaving spaces for rubrication to be added by hand. Rubrication was one of several steps in the medieval process of manuscript making. Those who called themselves rubricators were specialized scribes who received their text from the manuscript's original scribe and then embellished it with red ink to catch the eye.

The practice of rubrication was usually placed to mark the end of one section of text and the beginning of a new section. Headings were incorporated, such as pictures, and long, elaborate flourishes by the scribe were introduced to bring a manuscript more distinction. In beautiful illuminated manuscripts of the period, the areas at the beginnings of paragraphs are what are known as rubrication.

In March 1455, the future Pope Pius II wrote a letter saying he had seen pages from the Gutenberg Bible. It was being promoted and on display in Frankfurt. The 1455 letter cites sources for there being between 160 and 185 copies printed. Most of the copies, about three-quarters, were printed on paper, the rest was printed on vellum.

Some sources say that there were initially 180 bibles printed, and they took three years to produce.

Gutenberg's early printing endeavors, including what tests he may have used when creating his movable type printing press, are not very well known. His later works, including his bibles, were printed in such a way as to have required large quantities of type. There are those who speculate he may have used 100,000 individual sorts. Setting a page, for instance, would take half a day. Then there was all of the work in loading the press itself, inking the type, pulling the impressions, hanging up the sheets to dry, and distributing the type; this was a gargantuan project for anyone and would have taken days, if not weeks.

Gutenberg never wrote down his methods for how he printed his books. In the decades to come, punches and copper matrices were being used, as printing presses were everywhere in Europe by this time, but whether or not Gutenberg had used these is anybody's guess. What follows is a standard process for making type: a soft copper bar is used and a letter is carved, back to front, into it. This creates a matrix. This letter is then placed into a handheld mold, and a piece of type, or "sort," is cast by filling the mold with a metal; after cooling, the letter can be removed from the mold. The matrix can then be used and re-used to make hundreds or thousands of identical sorts so that the same character appearing anywhere in the book will look exactly alike. This uniformity of characters gave way over time to the development of fonts.

After casting, the sorts are arranged into type-cases, and these are used to make up pages which are then inked and printed. This procedure can also be repeated as needed. The sorts can be reused in any combination, and that is where the term "movable type" gets its name.

Gutenberg has long been credited with the making of types with punch, matrix, and mold. Recent evidence suggests that if he used the punch and matrix method, then all of his letters should have been nearly identical. The type used in his earliest works, however, show many variations due to miscasting and inking.

Chapter Seven

Gutenberg's Printed Books

"It is a press, certainly, but a press from which shall flow in inexhaustible streams Through it, God will spread His Word. A spring of truth shall flow from it; like a new start it shall scatter the darkness of ignorance, and cause a light heretofore unknown to shine amongst men."

—Johannes Gutenberg

In 1455, Gutenberg completed his 42-line Bible, known as the Gutenberg Bible. The Gutenberg Bible was the first major book printed using mass-produced movable metal type in Europe. Written in Latin, the Catholic Gutenberg Bible was a late fourth-century Latin translation of the Bible. In Gutenberg's time, the *Vulgate* was what the Church used.

Since Gutenberg's Bible was published, 49 copies have survived, and book lovers are in awe of the absolute beauty of the Bible itself. Without a doubt, these books are some of the most valuable in the world today.

As for the pages, the paper size is double folio with two pages printed on each side. This would be four pages per sheet. After printing, the paper was folded to the size of a single page. Usually what was done was that five of these folded sheets (which were 10 leaves or 20 printed pages) were combined into a single section called a quinternion. Sections could have as few as 4 leaves or as many as 12 leaves. Then, sections could be combined into books. Some sections may have been printed in larger quantities than others, especially the ones printed later in the publishing process, and they may even have been sold separately. Pages were not numbered.

This method was not new since this technique had been used to make blank white-paper books to be written afterward. What was new here was determining beforehand the correct placement and orientation of each page and how they would look on the five sheets that would result in the correct sequence, once they were printed.

The folio or page size had the ratio of 1.45:1. The printed area always had the same ratio and was shifted out of the middle to leave a 2:1 white margin. This white margin was both vertical and horizontal. It seems nothing was left to chance; historian John Man writes that the ratio was chosen to be close to the golden ratio of 1.61:1. The golden ratio has been used through history by, for example, Pythagoras and Euclid in ancient Greece, Medieval mathematicians, and Renaissance scientists.

A single complete copy of the Gutenberg Bible has 1,286 pages and is usually bound in two volumes. There are 4 pages per folio-sheet, 322 sheets of paper are required for each copy. The handmade paper that Gutenberg used was imported from Italy and of the highest quality. There is a watermark left by the papermold on each sheet.

The inks used by scribes in Gutenberg's time were water-based. Gutenberg developed an oil-based ink which stuck to his metal type better than the water ink. His ink was primarily carbon and had a high metallic content, with large amounts of copper, lead, and titanium. If you look closely at the pages of the Gutenberg Bible, the surface will appear to be very shiny. Gutenberg's ink really wasn't an ink; it was more like a varnish. What is called "printer's ink" is a varnish, and that means it sticks to its surface.

Gutenberg's idea was to use a single, hand-carved character to create identical copies of itself. Cutting just one letter could take one of his craftsmen a whole day of work. A single page using 2,500 letters made this way impossible. Copies were produced, and that's where the matrix took over. The matrix, once made, could be used over and over again. This piece of type could be put in a line, facing up, with other pieces of similar type. These lines were arranged to form blocks of text which could then be inked and pressed against paper. The desired text would be transferred to paper, hopefully without any misspellings.

Each unique character that Gutenberg created needed a master piece of type in order to be replicated. Each letter had uppercase and lowercase forms. Including the various punctuation marks, the Gutenberg Bible needed a set of 290 master characters. With this master set, it seems that six pages, containing 15,600 characters altogether, could be set at any one moment.

The Gutenberg Bible is printed in the blackletter type styles known as Textura and Schwabacher. The texture of the printed page was straight strokes up and down, combined with horizontal lines, giving the impression of a woven structure. Gutenberg was familiar with the technique of justification; he created a vertical, not an indented alignment at the left and right-hand sides of the column. He would use characters of narrower widths, add extra spaces around punctuation, and vary the width of spaces around words. Gutenberg also employed hanging punctuation, which meant that quotation marks, for instance, were outside of the block quote, thereby not interfering in how those characters were printed.

At first, the rubrics, or the headings used before each book of the Bible, were printed. Gutenberg quickly stopped doing this and allowed for gaps in the printing where the rubrication could be applied by hand. In this instance, he did come up with a guide on how to do this, one of which still survives.

Now that there was room left for the rubrics, beautiful illumination was what you saw in the early Gutenberg Bibles. The amount of decoration depended on how much a buyer was willing to pay for it. Some copies were never decorated. The vellum bibles were the most expensive of all. Many Gutenberg bibles have been rebound over the years, and approximately nine copies retain fifteenth-century bindings. Most of the copies were bound in Mainz or Erfurt. Most copies were divided into two volumes, the first volume ending with the Book of Psalms.

Sometime in 1456, tensions arose between Gutenberg and Fust, and Fust suddenly demanded all of his money back. He accused Gutenberg of misusing his funds, although what he thought the money was to be used for was not stated. By this time, Gutenberg's debt for printing the Bible was 20,000 guilders.

It was to the archbishop's court that Fust raised his lawsuit. A November 1455 legal document records that there had been a partnership for "the project of the books," and Fust maintained that Gutenberg had used the funds for other things. The court decided in favor of Fust, giving him control over the Bible printing workshop as well as half of all printed Bibles.

These court proceedings left Gutenberg bankrupt. To his credit, he either restarted or retained a small printing shop, and he was able to print a copy of a Bible for the town of Bamberg in 1459. Since his name never appeared on any of his printed works, many historians dispute what some say were Gutenberg's and what others say were not. Today you cannot even imagine writing or printing something without including your name. Such were the ways of the Middle Ages; beautiful statues and stonework in cathedrals, stained glass windows, and even early printing did not carry the names of the people who created these works.

In 1455, Gutenberg completed copies of a Bible with 42 lines on each page. Copies sold for 30 florins each. This would amount to three years' wages for one of his clerks. But, this was cheaper than a manuscript Bible which could take a scribe over a year to complete. Already,

Gutenberg's printing press was making an impact. His press was to bring a whole new world to Europe. The first printed books were religious in nature, because that is what most medieval books were at the dawn of the printing age. Those early printed books looked an awful lot like handwritten manuscripts too; that was done on purpose, so people could accept this new revolutionary way of copying books.

What happened when using the printing press was that the press soon changed the forms and uses of books in radical ways. As more and more books were getting printed, they stopped looking like those written manuscript forms with lined paper. More and more books were no longer religious tomes. Now every subject under the sun was starting to be printed; topics such as grammar, etiquette, and science were opening up an entire world to the middle and lower classes, who before this had no books to call their own.

By 1482, a mere 30 years from when Gutenberg set up his printing press, there were 100 printing presses in Western Europe. To break it down even further, there were 50 presses in Italy, 30 in the German states, 9 in France, 8 each in Spain and Holland, and 4 in England.

The middle and lower classes didn't really want expensive, heavy volumes of the Bible or other religious books; what they were happiest with was smaller, cheaper, and easier-to-use books. Aldus Manutius, an Italian printer and publisher, began publishing his pocket books. He went even further and revolutionized book publishing when he focused on these small editions and nothing else.

Manutius helped with spreading translations of the Greek classics, which helped to spread knowledge throughout Italy like nothing else. By 1500, there were over 40,000 different editions of the classics and over 6,000,000 copies in print.

Almost overnight, the printing press had dramatic effects on European civilization. The first effect was that knowledge could be given to people far and near. The information from books was quick and reliable. Because there were new books being printed in your town or city, people wanted to learn how to read. Books were the number one disseminator of knowledge. Now a wider reading public could be found wherever you went.

Printing had two main impacts on European society at large; first, with more and more books being printed, secular books were becoming increasingly popular. Now, scientists who were living in different parts of Europe could all work on the same problem at the same time, courtesy of the printed books. They could take the information they were seeing in books and expound on it, writing their advanced opinions on a subject and seeing it in print for everyone to learn about. Within one hundred years, this information-sharing would lead to the Scientific Revolution of the Enlightenment. This would radically change how Europeans looked at themselves and how they were beginning to understand their universe.

The second impact that printing had on European society was that it took book copying out of the hands of Church members; scribes were no longer needed to sit for weeks and months on end, copying religious books. Just this move alone made it very difficult for the Church to exert its control on the average citizen.

It was a mere 70 years after Gutenberg began using his printing press that Martin Luther nailed his *95 Theses* to the church door in Wittenberg. Luther was very familiar with the power of the written word, and he used it to his best ability.

Historians will tell you that the printing press is the most important invention between the invention of writing itself and today's modern computers. Not everyone will agree with that statement, but the printing press that Johannes Gutenberg unleashed on his world in Europe in 1450 was to have gigantic ramifications.

Chapter Eight

Later Life and Death

"Leisure without books is death, and burial of a man alive."

—Seneca

By 1462, Gutenberg was getting on in age. He had returned to Mainz and was happy living there until a diocesan feud found trouble for him yet again.

Back in 1459, Diether of Isenburg had been elected the new archbishop of Mainz. He barely beat out Adolph of Nassau. Diether formed alliances, ones which were not popular with the Pope, while Adolph of Nassau had his own alliances. Pope Pius II sought the replacement of Diether. He banished him in 1461, declaring him deposed, and Adolph of Nassau was appointed as the new archbishop of Mainz. There was just one small problem with this: the city of Mainz continued to support Diether, and he refused to vacate his post. Battles were fought on both sides, costing many lives and creating great devastation of all the settlements. The city of Mainz suffered tremendous damage. Eventually, Diether relinquished his position, and Adolph of Nassau became archbishop.

During these troubles, Gutenberg was exiled by Nassau. He moved once again to Eltville, where he may have set up shop with a new printing press belonging to the brothers Bechtermunze. In January 1465, Gutenberg's achievements were at last recognized, and he was given the title "Hofmann," or gentleman of the court. This honor included an annual court outfit, a stipend, 2,180 liters of grain, and 2,000 liters of wine, tax-free. He may have moved back to Mainz at this time.

In 1468, Johannes Gutenberg died and was buried in the Franciscan church in Mainz. The church and the cemetery were eventually destroyed, and Gutenberg's grave is lost for all time.

Chapter Nine

The Legacy of Johannes Gutenberg

"We can put television in its proper lighting by supposing that Gutenberg's great invention had been directed at printing only comic books."

—Robert M. Hutchins

When the Church didn't like things, and when people came up with manuscripts on their own to show around the village or town, these would be quickly scooped up and burned, as in the case of the Hussite crisis in the early 1400s. The Hussites were a Christian movement in the Bohemian Kingdom, and they were avid followers of a Czech reformer, Jan Hus.

Hus was one of a handful of church reformers, who were forerunners of the Protestant Reformation. They popped up, here and there, in history, each beginning to challenge Church teachings. In the case of the Hussites, when the authorities finally caught up with Hus and his cohorts, over 200 manuscripts of heretical writings were ordered to be burned. Jan Hus himself was burned at the stake in 1415 for being a heretic.

There was no easy way to spread your message in the early 1400s. People could talk about an issue as they traveled from place to place, but talk only went so far. Within one hundred years, all that would change. But had Johannes Gutenberg been born in the year 1000, the events and tools he needed to create his printing press would not have been available to him. In order for any invention to have a full impact on society and the world, the right conditions, at the right time, need to be in place. The printing press wasn't just the result of one man. It had been around before Johannes Gutenberg, only in lesser ways. Printing, as we have seen, was a combination of several different inventions and innovations: block-printing, rag paper, oil-based ink, interchangeable metal type, and the squeeze press. The catalyst behind all of this was Johannes Gutenberg.

Today's processes for printing are vastly different from what Johannes Gutenberg began with. Everything was done by hand, while now, a computer can assemble those same characters in a matter of seconds. In our modern world, there are more words being printed every second than were every year in the fifteenth and sixteenth centuries.

By the late eighteenth century and early nineteenth century, inventors began to improve on the printing presses they were using. The first modification was that metal was much better than wood to withstand use. By 1800, Earl Stanhope of England had created a printing press with a cast-iron frame. This Stanhope Press was the first of its kind made out of cast-iron. The Earl even added additional levers, which gave the printer more power. This press created cleaner, more powerful impressions, which were perfect for printing woodcuts and larger formats.

The Colombian Press, invented by George Clymer of Philadelphia, was also an iron-held press. This press could print 250 copies per hour. This press used a series of weights and counter-weights to increase the force of the impression and raise the platen (a flat plate of metal that presses the paper onto the form) after each impression.

In 1824, Daniel Treadwell of Boston was the first person to try and mechanize printing. He added gears and additional power to a wooden-framed platen, which made it four times faster than a handheld press. This press was in use for most of the nineteenth century.

Back in 1812, Fredrik Koenig had invented the steam-driven printing process. The Koenig Press could print 400 sheets per hour. Richard Hoe, an American press maker, made improvements to the Koenig Press, and he designed the Single Small Cylinder Press in 1832. Cylinder presses were much faster than platen and hand presses, and you could print 1,000 to 4,000 impressions an hour.

Presses kept getting faster and more precise. In 1865, William Bullock invented the Bullock Press which was the first press to use a continuous roll of paper. Once threaded into the machine, printing could be done on both sides at once. This press could print up to 12,000 sheets per hour, and later models could print 30,000 or more pages per hour.

But just like in Gutenberg's time, all type was still set and composed by hand. Monotype and Linotype machines would change the printing process because for the first time these machines would use mechanical means to set type.

In a Linotype machine, an operator would type on a keyboard similar to a typewriter which produced a perforated band of paper. This band was then decoded by a machine that cast type from hot metal. These machines could cast a whole row of type at a time, and if the operator made a mistake, the entire line would have to be retyped and recast.

The Monotype machine was very similar to the Linotype machine. Again, an operator would type out text that would be captured on a perforated tape. Then the operator tore off the tape and ran it through a separate casting machine which produced a mold containing matrices for each character that had been typed. Monotype was easier to correct than Linotype machines, and they created a finer quality type, which was usually preferred in the book publishing trade.

Then computers revolutionized everything. Now, you can be your own author, editor, printer, and compositor right from the comfort of home. Software has been developed which has made the world of printing a digital one.

Printing has come a long way since those early examples in Gutenberg's day. Johannes Gutenberg had a dream to make printing available and accessible for everyone. Many would agree that he succeeded.

Conclusion

When the first digital books appeared, most publishers were convinced that this spelled the end to traditional printing. People would no longer want a book in their hand as they could download one to a device and read it at their leisure. We now know that this didn't happen; both modes of printing have settled comfortably into their own venues, and both continue to attract their adherents.

Gutenberg's printing press revolutionized not only his world but ours as well. Even those who know next to nothing about printing have heard of Johannes Gutenberg and his printing press. When printers and publishers went looking for a venue to collect books into, they settled on Project Gutenberg, the largest and oldest digital library.

Johannes Gutenberg has proved to be one of history's most influential people of all time. Remember, he was not successful in his own lifetime; struggling to find funds for his projects, running into people who took everything away from him. The one thing they couldn't take away was Gutenberg's expertise, which created a legacy that lasts until this day.

Made in the USA
Las Vegas, NV
18 April 2022